ADVENTURES IN NATURE

WILD FLOWERS

Jen Green

PowerKiDS
press™

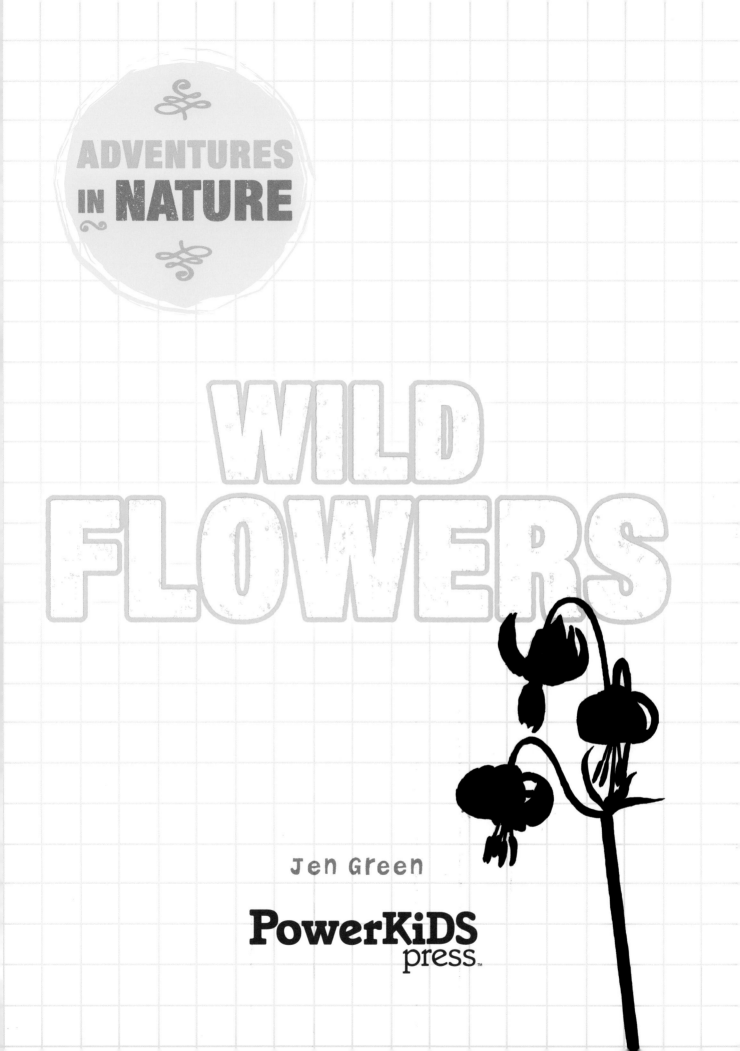

Published in 2016 by
The Rosen Publishing Group, Inc.
29 East 21st Street, New York, NY 10010

Cataloging-in-Publication Data
Green, Jen.
Wild flowers / by Jen Green.
p. cm. — (Adventures in nature)
Includes index.
ISBN 978-1-5081-4594-3 (pbk.)
ISBN 978-1-5081-4595-0 (6-pack)
ISBN 978-1-5081-4596-7 (library binding)
1. Wild flowers — Juvenile literature. 2. Wild flowers —
Identification — Juvenile literature. I. Green, Jen. II. Title.
QK49.G74 2016
582.13—d23

Copyright © 2016 Watts/PowerKids

Series Editor: Sarah Peutrill
Series Designer: Matt Lilly
Picture researcher: Kathy Lockley

Picture Credits: Alamy/Robert Clay 11B; Dreamstime.com/Alex
Scott 8TR, Alinamd 23, Alon79 6T, American Spirit 6B, Andrew
Roland 25BL, Anette Linnea Rasmussen 8CL, Annestaub 5RC,
Artem Podobedov ContentsC, 16B, Carolyn Morrison 26B,
Christopher Smith 29TL, Dieonis 8L, Elena Elisseeva 10B,
Kamlesh Sethy 5TR, Konradweiss 25TL, Lawrence Weslowski Jr
18B, Linda Bair 7C, Linda Macpherson 13, Mykola Ivashchenko
18T, Patrick Wang 25BR, Paul Lawrence 7TL, Simon Gurney
25BC, Skimerlin 14B, sunheyy 5C, Tikta Alik 5BL, Tyler Olson
7TR, 21LC, Venkra 29TC, Youths 29TR; FLPA/Kevin Elsby 25TC;
iStockphoto.com/dennisvdw 28T; Photoshot/Picture Alliance/
Layer,W 14T; Science Photo Library/Cordelia Molloy 8BR;
Shutterstock.com /2009fotofriends 19TR, Alina Reynbakh 24C,
Andrew F. Kazmierski 21BR, artoflightpro 19LC, BestPhotoPlus
4L, BestPhotoStudio 19RC, Bildagentur Zoonar GmbH 5BC,
27TC, 27TL, 27BR, BMJ 17CR, Butterfly Hunter ContentsB,
26T, Chrislofotos 7BL, Dancestrokes 15T, Diana Taliun 7RC,
duvduv 17TC, Elenamiv Front Cover, F_studio 12T, Fotofermer
ContentsT, 12B, G10ck 17TL, Gio.tto 7LC, GSD Photography
22, H Helene 28B, Incredible Arctic 27BL, irin-k 5BR, Jakkrit
Orrasri 24BR, Joseph Scott Photography 17BL, Karin Jaehne
24TL, Kristina Postnikova 5LC, Kseniia Perminova 4R, Kucher
Sernil 19BR, KYTan 17BR, Lorraine Hudgins 16T, Lostry7 8CR,
Margo Harrison 11T, MarkMirror 20B, 27TR, Martin Fowler 8C,
20T, oksana2010 29BR, panyajampatong 21C, Paul Nash 25TR,
pavels 29RC, PHOTOFUN 21e, picturepartners 21TL, Pospisil
15B, Potapov Alexander 10T, prizzz 29C, Rainbohm 27BC,
Roxana Bashyrova 17C, Ruud Morijn Photographer 21TR, Sherri
R. Camp 19TL, Sombra 7TC, Stefan Holm 9, tkemot 21RC, tr3gin
21c, Tsekhmister 15L, Zont 17TR z

Manufactured in the United States of America

CPSIA Compliance Information: Batch #BW16PK: For Further Information contact
Rosen Publishing, New York, New York at 1-800-237-9932

Can you find SIX daisies hidden on the pages?

Clara is out looking for wild flowers. Can you find her?

There are lots more puzzles in this book. You can solve them by reading the text or by looking closely at the photos. The answers are on page 30.

Contents

What are wild flowers? 4

Shapes and sizes 6

Color and scent 8

How do wild flowers live? 10

Parts of a flower 12

Passing pollen 14

Fruits and seeds 16

Wild flower cycles 18

Woodland flowers 20

Grasslands and meadows 22

Living by water 24

Extreme places 26

Towns and cities 28

Puzzle answers 30

Glossary 31

Index and websites 32

what are wild flowers?

Bright and beautiful, wild flowers grow naturally all over the world. Wild flowers are plants, living things that can make their own food. Different types of wild flowers grow in the desert, up mountains, in woodland, or by the sea. When they flower, they bring color to our world.

All garden flowers were originally wild flowers growing somewhere in the world.

Using a magnifying glass can help you examine flowers up close.

This book will help you explore the wonderful world of flowers. When you go flower hunting, take a notebook and colored pens or pencils to record what you see. A wild flower book will help you identify your finds. A magnifying glass and camera can also come in handy. Good luck on the wild flower challenge!

Wild flower family

Wild flowers belong to the huge family of flowering plants that includes grasses, shrubs such as roses, and broad-leaved trees such as oak and apple. All of these plants have flowers and reproduce by making seeds. However not all plants reproduce in this way. Conifer trees produce seeds in cones, not flowers, and ferns reproduce using spores, not seeds.

cherry tree in blossom

Spot the flowering plants

Which of these are flowering plants?

apple
tree

tulip

fern

mallow

conifer
tree

daisy

5

Shapes and Sizes

There are thousands of wild flower species, and no two look exactly alike. Many wild flowers are tiny, and you need a magnifying glass to see the very smallest. The very biggest measure over 3 feet (1 m) across!

Flower shapes are amazingly varied. They may be shaped like stars, crosses, bells, or trumpets. Some flowers are flat like saucers, others are rounded. Some flowers have their own stem. In other species, the stem carries a cluster of small flowers or forms a long spike of flowers.

Sunflower heads can measure 20 inches (50 cm) across.

Orange poppies produce a single flower. Blue lupines produce a tall spike of flowers.

Flower types

Which of these have single flowers on a stem and which have many flowers on one stem?

bindweed

buttercup

columbine

harebell

lupine

Turk's cap lily

early purple orchid

THE flower HUNT CHALLENGE

Get drawing

When you find a flower you don't know, make a sketch. Describe the color, shape and structure of petals and leaves. Write down the date and where you saw it. Then try to find it in a wild flower book.

color and scent

Wild flowers have many beautiful colors – pale or deep yellow, sky-blue, rosy red, orange, pink, white, and purple. Some flowers are green, which makes them hard to see, while others have several different colors. Many plant books group flowers by color, which makes it easy to identify new flowers.

white campion

marsh marigold

forget-me-not

scarlet pimpernel

mallow

Many wild flowers are scented. The smell comes from petals or a sweet juice called nectar. Colors, scents, and nectar attract animals such as insects, which help plants to reproduce. Some flowers release scent at night to attract night-flying moths and bats.

Many flowers have markings which only show up in ultraviolet light. Humans can't see this light, but insects can. The markings guide insects to the nectar in the center of the flower.

Outlines

Copy these outlines carefully and use the photos on the left to color them correctly.

mallow

white campion

scarlet pimpernel

forget-me-not

marsh marigold

THE flower HUNT CHALLENGE

Smell different flowers*

....

Which is your favorite scent?

harebell

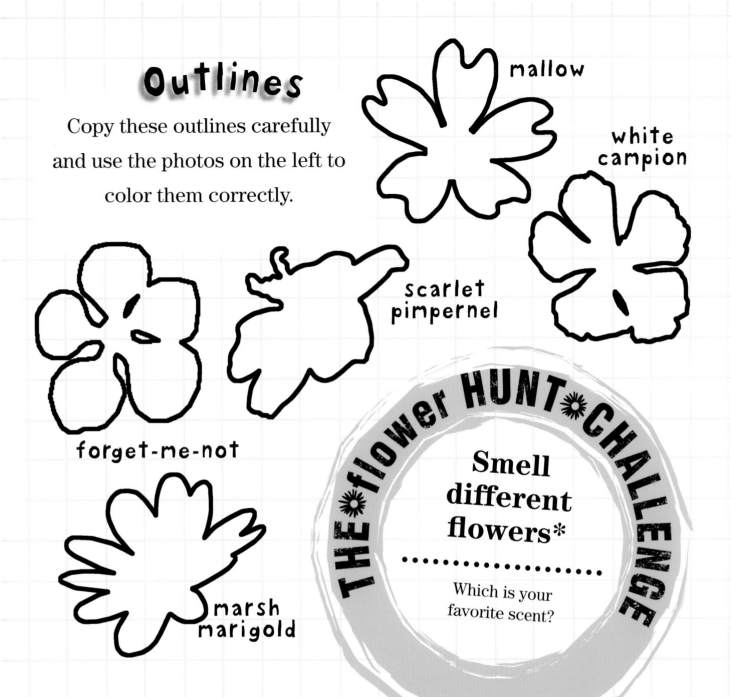

Flower names

Some flower names refer to their color, shape or scent. Sweet William is sweetly scented. Harebells and bluebells are named after their bell-shaped flowers. Can you guess the color and shape of buttercups?

*As long as you don't have any known allergies!

How do wild flowers live?

All wild flowers have the same basic parts: roots, stems, leaves, and flowers. Roots anchor the plant in the soil and soak up moisture. The stem supports the flower and transports food and water around the plant. Green leaves make the plant's food.

A plant's leaves absorb sunlight energy. This energy is used to transform water and nutrients from the soil and carbon dioxide gas from the air into sugary food, which the plant uses to grow. This process is called photosynthesis.

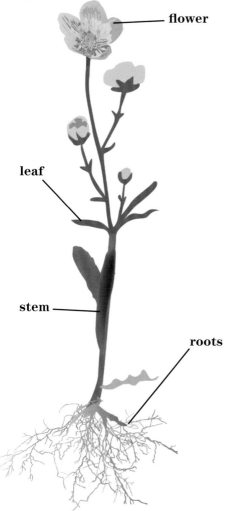

flower

leaf

stem

roots

The parts of a buttercup

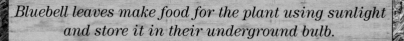

Bluebell leaves make food for the plant using sunlight and store it in their underground bulb.

Flower changes

Flowers play a vital part in the plant's life cycle but don't usually last long. A flower begins as a tight bud, which opens and spreads its petals. Later the petals wither and drop off. This can take weeks, a few days or just a day.

Poppy parts

Place these pictures of a poppy in the right order. (See the stages below for clues.)

b

c

d

a

e

1. Poppy bud
2. Flower starts to open
3. Fully open
4. Petals drop off
5. Ripe seed pod

THE flower HUNT CHALLENGE

Study changes

Find a wild flower and observe it over several days. Can you describe what happens?

parts of a flower

All wild flowers have petals, sepals and the male and female parts used to make seeds. Sepals are like green petals. They protect the flower before it opens. The petals surround the center which contains the reproductive parts. In flowers such as harebells and foxgloves, the petals join to make a tube.

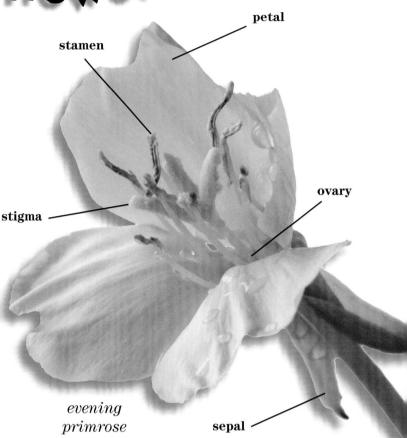

petal

stamen

ovary

stigma

sepal

evening primrose

At the center of most flowers are several stalks with knobby tips.

stigma

hibiscus

These are the male stamens which produce pollen. The dusty grains of pollen on the tips contain the male sex cells. In the very center is another stalk with a sticky tip. This is the female part, called the stigma. At the base of this stalk is the ovary, which contains the ovules. These are the female egg cells which will grow into seeds.

close up

Use a magnifying glass to take a close look at flowers. Most flowers have both male and female parts, but some have either one or the other. Can you spot any of these?

flower parts

Parts such as stamens and stigma look different on different flowers. Can you figure out what a, b, and c are on this flower?

a

b

c

THE flower HUNT CHALLENGE

Draw a single flower

Make a large drawing of your flower. Add color using crayons or colored pencils.

passing pollen

Before wild flowers can make seeds, pollen from one flower must pass to the stigma of another. The transfer of pollen is called pollination.

Plants such as grasses and nettles use wind to spread their pollen. Some plants that grow in or by ponds and streams use water to spread their pollen.

Many wild flowers use bees, butterflies, and other insects as pollinators. Honeybees visit

Hazel catkins release pollen that blows away on the wind.

flowers to collect nectar and pollen. When a bee lands on a flower, pollen from the stamens sticks to its hairy body. Then it visits a second flower, where some of the pollen grains rub off on the flower's stigma. Now the male sex cells from the pollen find their way to the ovary and join with the ovules. This is called fertilization and it allows the plant to make seeds.

A honeybee collects pollen and stores it in little pouches on its legs.

14

Pollination mix-up

These three photos showing pollination have been put in the wrong order. Look closely and put them in the right order. Use the numbered clues to help you.

a

b

clues:

1. Arriving at flower

2. Entering flower getting covered with pollen

3. Arriving at second flower, covered in pollen

c

THE flower HUNT CHALLENGE

Become a pollination detective!

Watch what happens when insects visit flowers.

Fruits and seeds

After fertilization wild flowers drop their petals. The ovary at the base of the flower swells to become a fleshy fruit, such as a cherry or blackberry. Some fruits called nuts have a hard case. Fruits and nuts protect the fertilized ovules inside while they ripen into seeds.

Wild flowers need to spread their seeds far and wide, to places where there is light and space for the young plants to grow. Milkweed, thistles, and dandelions produce light seeds that blow away on the wind. Some water plants produce floating seeds that drift downstream with the current.

This waxwing is eating rose hips.

Many plants use animals to spread their seeds. Juicy fruits such as rose hips and blackberries are eaten by birds and mammals. The seeds pass right through their bodies and are deposited in their droppings. Flowers such as burdock produce hooked seeds that catch in animal fur and are carried far away.

burdock seed with hooks

16

Fruits and flowers

Match these well-known fruits or seeds with their flowers.

a

b

blackberry

thistledown

rose hip

c

Germination

Seeds that land in warm, sunny soil start to grow, or germinate. The seed case splits open and a little root grows downward. Meanwhile a green shoot grows upward. The new plant spreads its leaves and starts to photosynthesize and grow.

A seedling begins to grow.

Wild flower cycles

periwinkle

In cool and temperate parts of the world, wild flowers have a yearly cycle that matches the seasons. In spring they grow fresh leaves and buds. Most bloom in either spring or summer, and produce fruits and seeds in autumn. During the cold months of winter the green parts die back. Some plants die, leaving their seeds to sprout in spring. Others, such as crocuses and lilies, survive by storing food in underground parts called bulbs and corms.

All over the world, wild flowers bloom in certain seasons. For example, wood anemones, violets, and daffodils are a sign of spring. Purple loosestrife, rosebay willowherb, and dog rose flower in summer. Michaelmas daisies and bindweed are still flowering in autumn, while snowdrops and some periwinkles start to flower in winter.

Spring flowers in North America.

Seasonal puzzle

Match these wild flowers to their season.

purple loosestrife

daffodil

snowdrop

Michaelmas daisy

spring   summer   autumn   winter

Daily cycles

daisy

Many flowers have a daily cycle too – they open their petals by day and close them at night. Daisies only open their petals fully if the weather is sunny. This plant was once called a day's eye, which was later shortened to daisy.

Woodland flowers

Some flowers grow almost anywhere, but most are suited to a particular habitat, such as a woodland. Woodland flowers mostly bloom in spring, when broad-leaved trees are not in full leaf. This allows light and moisture to reach plants growing under trees. In spring, woods are great places to look for wild flowers such as primroses, bluebells, and wood anemones. Foxgloves don't mind the shade and flower in summer.

Yellow archangel blooms in summer.

Wood anemones carpet woodlands in spring.

foxglove

wild geranium

a

Flower matching

Look closely at these
flower parts – which flowers do
they come from?

e

b

c

d

buttercup

wild ginger

periwinkle

Woodland climbers

Woodland plants such as ivy and
honeysuckle reach the light by climbing
trees and shrubs. Honeysuckle winds
its long, tough stems around shrubs and
saplings. Ivy scrambles up trees by putting
out root-like suckers which cling to the bark.

*Ivy clings to
a tree trunk.*

21

grasslands and meadows

Wild grasslands and meadows are a mass of flowers in spring and summer. Flowers such as lupines and poppies are quite large, but others are tiny, so you need to look carefully to find them. Meadow flowers also bloom by the sides of roads and railways.

Wild grasslands once covered most of Europe and North America, but these were mostly plowed up long ago to make fields for crops. Wild flowers can still flourish in fields, but many farmers use poison or use chemicals to kill wild flowers.

Many different flowers grow in a meadow in North America. You can study plants in a lawn or meadow by marking a square using pegs and string. Count how many of each wild flower is in the square. Use a flower book to identify the plants.

Spot the flowers

How many different types of wild flowers can you spot in this meadow?

THE flower HUNT CHALLENGE

Photo time

Photograph the wild flowers you see growing in a hedge or meadow. Hold the camera steady to take close-up photos.

Living by water

All plants need water, but some like it so much they live in or by rivers, streams, and ponds, and can't survive in drier places.

Be careful by the water's edge when you are spotting water plants.

Duckweed is one of the world's smallest plants. These tiny plants float in ponds, where they spread out over the surface. Each plant has a tiny root that absorbs nutrients.

Bullrushes growing by a river

A frog rests on a water lily.

Tall plants, such as reeds, bulrushes and flag iris, grow along the banks of ponds and streams. Other plants grow in the water, either floating at the surface or underwater. Water lilies have roots in the pond mud and spread their floating leaves and flowers on the surface.

Seaside plants

Wild flowers also live at the seaside, where they have to cope with gale-force winds and salty spray. Salt dries plants out, so flowers such as sea kale and sea holly have waxy leaves that keep in moisture. Seaside plants also have long roots which anchor them among the rocks on cliffs or in sand and pebbles on the beach.

match the habitats

Different habitats are found by the sea, such as cliffs, sand dunes and pebble beaches. Can you match these seaside flowers with their habitats?

sea sandwort

yellow horned poppy

sea pink

a

b

c

Extreme places

cactus flower

Wild flowers look delicate, but some are tough enough to thrive in very harsh places such as mountains, deserts, and the Arctic. Tundra and mountain plants cope with long, freezing winters when the ground is frozen. When spring finally comes, these plants grow quickly, flower, and produce seeds before summer ends and the cold returns.

Many tundra and mountain plants grow low to the ground. They grow in low, rounded cushions that provide protection from icy winds.

Deserts have extreme temperatures: boiling hot by day, but cold at night. The main problem here is lack of water. Plants such as cacti have long roots that soak up every last drop of moisture. They store the moisture in their swollen stems, which are covered with sharp spines to prevent them being nibbled by thirsty animals.

Identify the hardy flowers

Match the silhouettes to these hardy tundra and mountain flowers.

a   b   c   d   e   f

blue columbine

star-shaped mountain avens

globeflower

Arctic poppy

glacier lily

gentian

Deserts in bloom

When rain finally falls in a desert, seeds germinate quickly. For a few days the desert is a carpet of bright flowers which attract insect pollinators. After pollination, desert plants quickly produce seeds which survive when the water dries up, the plants die, and the desert becomes bare again.

Towns and cities

Towns and cities seem an unlikely habitat for wild flowers because so much of the ground is covered by brick and concrete. However, hardy plants such as dandelions, buddleia, and ragwort thrive in nooks and crannies. They sprout from brick walls, cracks in the pavement and on empty lots.

Butterflies flock to a buddleia bush growing on an empty lot.

Wild flowers also grow in parks and gardens. Here they are unpopular with gardeners who see them as weeds. However, weeds such as nettles, thistles, and brambles provide food and shelter for animals such as birds, mammals, frogs, and insects. You can give nature a helping hand by allowing wild flowers to flourish in one corner of the garden! Out in the countryside, you should never pick wild flowers.

Silverweed can grow in cracks in stones.

Name puzzle

Unscramble the names of six
wild flowers that thrive in cities:

c

noddenail

a

oxladfat

b

tragrow

d

rediweef

e

hetslit

f

letnet

THE flower HUNT CHALLENGE

Get planting

Help wild flowers by sowing
a packet of wild flower
seeds in a corner of
your garden or school
grounds.

Puzzle answers

5 Spot the flowering plants

apple tree; tulip; mallow; daisy

13 Flower parts

a – stigma
b – petal
c – stamen

11 Poppy parts

1. Poppy bud – a
2. Flower starts to open – c
3. Fully open – d
4. Petals drop off – b
5. Ripe seed pod – e

7 Flower types

single flowers: bindweed,
buttercup, columbine and
harebell
many flowers on one stem:
Turk's cap lily, early purple
orchid, and lupine

15 Pollination mix-up

b, a, c.

17 Fruits and flowers

blackberry – c
thistledown – b
rose hip – a

19 Seasonal puzzle

purple loosestrife – summer
daffodil – spring
snowdrop – winter
Michaelmas daisy – autumn

21 Flower matching

a – wild ginger
b – periwinkle
c – buttercup
d – wild geranium
e – foxglove

23 Spot the flowers

Seven different
flower types – but
you may spot more.

27 Identify the hardy flowers

a – gentian
b – star-shaped mountain avens
c – glacier lily
d – globeflower
e – blue columbine
f – Arctic poppy

25 Match the habitats

sea sandwort – b
yellow horned poppy – c
sea pink – a

29 Name puzzle

a – toadflax
b – ragwort
c – dandelion
d – fireweed
e – thistle
f – nettle

Glossary

broad-leaved tree Tree with wide leaves, rather than slim conifer needles, that sheds its leaves in autumn and grows them again in spring.

bulb Underground stem that stores food in plants such as daffodils.

carbon dioxide Gas in the air, which plants use to make their food.

conifer Type of tree that reproduces by producing cones containing seeds rather than flowers.

corm Underground stem that stores food in plants such as crocuses.

fertilization When male and female plant cells join so that a flower can make seeds.

floret Tiny flower which forms part of a flower head.

flowering plant Member of the large family of plants that produce flowers, fruits, and seeds.

germinate When a plant sprouts from a seed and starts to grow.

habitat Natural home of plants or animals, such as a woodland or meadow.

nectar Sugary liquid produced by flowers to attract insects.

nutrients Nourishment. Plants get nutrients from the soil.

ovary Female part at the base of a flower where the seeds are made.

ovule Female sex cell which becomes a seed after fertilization.

photosynthesis Process by which plants make their food using carbon dioxide, water, and sunlight energy.

pollen Tiny grains that contain the male sex cells of flowers.

pollination When pollen is transferred from one flower to another, to fertilize the second flower.

pollinator Animal, such as an insect, which helps to pollinate flowers.

reproduce To produce offspring. Flowering plants reproduce by making seeds.

seed Part of a plant that is able to grow into a new plant.

sepals Green, petal-like parts which protect flower buds.

shrub Woody plant that is smaller than a tree.

species Particular type of plant or animal, such as a snowdrop.

spores Tiny cells which ferns use to reproduce.

stamens Male parts of a flower which produce pollen. Stamens look like little stalks.

stigma Female part of a flower that receives pollen.

ultraviolet light Form of light that humans cannot see, but insects can.

Index

C

conifers 5

F

ferns 5
fertilization 14, 16
flower colors 7–10
flower shapes 6–7, 9
fruits 16–18

G

germination 17, 27

H

habitats 4, 20–29

I

insects 8, 14–15, 27–28

L

leaves 7, 10, 17–18, 20, 24–25

N

nectar 8, 14
nuts 16

P

parts of a flower 10–13, 21
photosynthesis 10, 17
pollen 12, 14–15
pollination 14–15, 27

R

reproduction 5, 8, 11–18, 26–27

S

scent 8–9
seasons 18–19
seeds 5, 11–12, 14, 16–18, 26–27

W

weeds 22, 28

Websites

PowerKids Press has developed an online list of websites related to the subject of this book. This site is updated regularly. Please use this link to access the list:
www.powerkidslinks.com/ain/wildflowers